Published by

Anders Publishing

4830 Wilson Road, Suite 156

Humble, TX 77396

●

"Meeting The Need"
Customer Service Training Manual

Developed by
Anders Consulting Group

Table of Contents

Customer Service Training

Customers today demand an unparalleled experience. Statistics show that most customers will become repeat customers if they receive the expected service. If the service they receive does not meet or exceed expectations, these customers will take their business elsewhere. Salespeople in stores and agents in call centers give the first impression of the company. These individuals possess a large amount of value in the company's presentation, perception, and business standards. Being the face and voice of the company weighs heavily in meeting the needs of ALL customers. Those who invest in their employees' success see the quick return on investment that customer service training provides.

If you want your customer service representatives to provide a world-class experience, then "Meeting A Need" is the answer you have been looking for. This customer service training seminar equips your staff with the tools and skills to communicate effectively and efficiently. Upon completing this seminar, you will be prepared to give all customers an unparalleled experience.

Upon completing this customer service training seminar includes:

- Improved customer satisfaction scores
- Reduced escalations
- Increased call resolution rates
- Positive energy
- A common service language
- Improved staff morale
- Reduced turnover
- Reduced costs

This customer service training seminar is perfect for anyone who provides service to internal or external customers, including representatives in:

- Customer service departments
- Inside sales and order desks
- Credit and collections
- Call Centers

Customer Service

What is Customer Service

Customer service relates to customer service before, during, and after a purchase. No matter the size of your business, excellent customer service must be at the heart of your business model if you wish to succeed. Providing good customer service to all potential, new, and existing customers is essential. Although it can take extra resources, time, and money, excellent customer service can generate positive word-of-mouth for your business, keep your customers happy, and encourage them to purchase from your company again. Good customer service can help your business grow and prosper.

Why is customer service important?

It can help you increase customer loyalty

- increase the amount of money each customer spends with your business

- increase how often a customer buys from you

- generate positive word-of-mouth and reputation

- decrease barriers to buying (for example, if your business has an excellent reputation of customer service for refunds, you are more likely to entice a hesitant buyer to purchase from you).

What is excellent customer service?

Excellent customer service is about:

- Treating your customers respectfully

- following up on feedback

- Handling complaints and returns gracefully

- Understanding your customers' needs and wants

- Exceeding customer expectations

- going out of your way to help them.

Communication

Effective communication skills are fundamental to success in many aspects of life. Many jobs require strong communication skills, and socially, people with improved communication skills usually enjoy better interpersonal relationships with friends and family. Effective communication is a critical interpersonal skill, and learning how to improve our communication has many benefits.

Focus on the meaning of what you want to communicate. Aim to increase understanding by considering how the other person might receive your message. Communicating clearly can help avoid misunderstandings and potential conflicts with others. By speaking eloquently, you will come across as more intelligent and mature. Be aware of the messages you send via non-verbal channels: make eye contact and avoid defensive body language. Present information in a way that its meaning can be clearly understood. Pay particular attention to cultural differences, past experiences, attitudes, and abilities before conveying your message. Avoid jargon and over-complicated language; explain things as simply as possible. Request clarification if unclear about a message. Always avoid racist and sexist terms or any language that may offend.

Know Your Customer

- Humor is always a good thing.

Laughing releases endorphins that can help relieve stress and anxiety; most people like to laugh and will feel drawn to somebody who can make them laugh. Don't be afraid to be funny or clever, but ensure your sense of Humor is appropriate to the situation. Use your sense of Humor to break the ice, lower barriers, and gain the affection of others. By using appropriate Humor, you will be perceived as more charismatic.

Be Consistent

- Treat People Equally

Always aim to communicate on an equal basis and avoid patronizing people. Please do not talk about others behind their backs and try not to develop favorites: treating people as your equals will build trust and respect. Check that people understand your words to avoid confusion and negative feelings. Encourage open and honest feedback from the receiver to ensure your message is understood and to prevent the receiver from feeding back what they think you want to hear. If confidentiality is an issue, make sure its boundaries are known and ensure its maintenance.

Few people want to be around someone who is frequently miserable. Do your best to be friendly, upbeat, and positive with other people. Maintain a positive, cheerful attitude to your job: when things do not go to plan, stay optimistic and learn from your mistakes. People respond positively if you smile often and remain cheerful.

Understanding Your Customer

Understanding your customers' needs begins with delivering an unparalleled experience through your service. This is done by understanding your customers contact you for a specific reason. Individuals bring their car to a mechanic shop for repairs, right? Why do these same individuals not bring their vehicles to a graphic designer for the needed repairs? The mechanic would be the expert and proper person to meet the auto repair needs. With this said, your customers only call you because you are the expert. You are the individual who can meet their demand, resolve their problem, and or provide the necessary information to get the job done. This is only executed by you being enthused to assist your customers. It will be up to you to turn your customers into clients. Customers discern when you are being genuine with your efforts. Every customer will be different, and how you connect with that customer is critical. That is why The Connect is so essential. The Connect seminar is to focus on how to communicate with customers. At the end of the training seminar, you will be able to understand the importance of connecting with customers, identify effective methods for making good connections, and communicate well to ensure successful interaction with customers.

The Four Social Styles and How You Should Negotiate With Them

The Intimidator

Let us begin by looking at the characteristics of the Intimidator. Intimidators are action and goal-driven, need to see results, and have a quick reaction time. They are decisive, independent, disciplined, practical, and efficient. They typically use facts and data, speak and act quickly, lean forward, point, and make direct eye contact. Their body posture is often rigid, and they have controlled facial expressions.

They rarely want to waste time on personal talk or preliminaries and can be perceived by another style as dominating or harsh and severe in pursuit of a goal. They are comfortable in positions of power and control and have businesslike offices with certificates and commendations on the wall. In times of stress, directors may become autocratic.

- Assertive but not responsive
- Task, rather than people-oriented
- Decisive and determined
- Controlled emotions
- Set on efficiency and effectiveness
- Likes control, often in a hurry
- Firm, stable relationships
- Stubborn, tough
- Impatient
- Inflexible, poor listener

How To Negotiate With Intimidators:

- Plan to ask questions about and discuss specifics, actions, and results.
- Use facts and logic!
- When necessary, disagree with facts rather than opinions, and be assertive.
- Keep it businesslike, efficient, and to the point.
- Personal guarantees and testimonials are the least effective - it is better to provide options and facts.
- Do not invade personal space.

The Observer

Observers are concerned with being organized, having all the facts, and being careful before acting. They must be accurate, correct, precise, orderly, and organized and conform to standard operating procedures, organizational rules, and historical ways of doing things. They typically have a slow reaction time and work more slowly and carefully than Intimidators. They are perceived as severe, diligent, persistent, and exacting. Usually, they are task-oriented, use facts and data, speak slowly, lean back, and use their hands frequently. They do not make direct eye contact and control their facial expressions. Others may see them as stuffy, indecisive, critical, picky and moralistic. They are comfortable in positions where they can check facts and figures and be sure they are right. They have neat, well-organized offices, and Thinkers tend to avoid conflict in times of stress.

The Observer
- Not assertive, not responsive
- Precise, orderly, and businesslike
- Rational and cooperative
- Self-controlled and serious
- Motivated by logic and facts
- Not quick to make decisions
- Distrusts persuasive people
- Like things in writing and detail
- Security conscious
- Critical, aloof, skeptical
- Excellent problem solver
- Likes rigid timetables

To Negotiate With Observers:

- Act rather than words to demonstrate helpfulness and willingness.
- Stick to specifics.
- Observers expect salespeople to overstate.
- Their decisions are based on facts and logic, and they avoid risk.
- They can often be very cooperative, but established relationships take time.
- Consider telling them what the product will not do. They will respect you for it and have spotted the deficiencies anyway.
- Discuss reasons and ask 'why' questions.
- Become less responsive and less assertive yourself.

The Connector

Connectors need cooperation, personal Security, and acceptance. They are uncomfortable with and will avoid conflict at all costs. They value personal relationships, helping others, and being liked. Some Connectors will sacrifice their desires to win approval from others. They prefer to work with others in a team effort rather than individually, and they have an inhumed reaction time and little concern with effecting change. Typically, they are friendly, supportive, respectful, willing, dependable, and agreeable. They are also people-oriented.

They use opinions rather than facts and data, speak slowly and softly, and use more vocal inflection than Thinkers and Directors. They lean back while communicating and do not make direct eye contact; they also have casual postures and animated expressions. Other styles perceive them as conforming, unsure, pliable, dependent, and awkward. They have homely offices-family photographs, plants, etc. Connectors' reaction to stress is to comply with others.

The Connector
- Not assertive but responsive
- Dependent on others
- Respectful, willing, and agreeable
- Emotionally expressive
- Everyone's friend, supportive, soft-hearted
- Low risk taker, likes Security
- Group builder
- Over-sensitive
- Not goal-orientated

To Negotiate With Connectors:

- Work jointly to seek common ground.
- Find out about personal interests and family.
- Be patient and avoid going for what looks like an easy pushover.
- Use personal assurance and specific guarantees and avoid options and probabilities.
- Take time to be agreeable.
- Focus discussion on how.
- Demonstrate low-risk solutions.
- Please do not take advantage of their good nature.

The Socializer

Socializers enjoy involvement, excitement, and interpersonal action. They are friendly, stimulating, enthusiastic, and good at involving and motivating others. They are also ideas-oriented, have little concern for routine, are future-oriented, and usually have a quick reaction time. They need to be accepted by others and be spontaneous, outgoing, energetic, friendly, and focused on people rather than tasks. Typically, they use opinions and stories rather than facts and data. They speak and act quickly, vary vocal inflection, lean forward, point, and make direct eye contact.

They use their hands when talking and have a relaxed body posture and an animated expression. Their feelings often show on their faces; others perceive them as excitable, impulsive, undisciplined, and may have leisure equipment like golf clubs and tennis racquets. Under stressful conditions, Socializers tend to resort to personal attacks.

The Socializer
- Assertive and responsive
- Reactive, impulsive, decisions spontaneous, intuitive
- Placing more importance on relationships than tasks
- Emotionally expressive, sometimes dramatic
- Flexible agenda, short attention span, quickly loved
- Enthusiastic
- Strong persuasive skills, talkative and gregarious
- Optimistic, takes risks
- Creative

To Negotiate With Socializers:

- Seek opinions in an area you wish to develop to achieve mutual understanding.
- Discussion should be people, as well as fact-oriented.
- Keep summarizing and work out specifics on points of agreement.
- Try short, fast-moving experience stories.
- Make sure to pin them down in a friendly way.
- Remember to discuss the future as well as the present.
- Look out for the impulse buy.

Skill Practice

What did you notice?

What needed to be done correctly?

What could have been done?

The Connect

How do you make The Connect?

Before you begin trying to sell, ask probing questions to your customer. Ask only questions that will help your customer explain why they are there. "Once you can gather this information, it is time for you to show your expertise. This is the time to show why your product and or service can and will satisfy their need. "Probing questions are fundamental to relationship building, and the more skilled you are at utilizing open and closed-ended questions, the stronger the relationship you will be able to create."

Why "The Connect" is important

- Connecting with customers is the basis for all successful customer relationships.

- Connecting with customers allows customer service, customer care, call center, and retail staff to understand their customers better and to find more ways to meet their needs and fulfill their requirements.

- When representatives connect with their customers, they create satisfied, loyal customers who will keep doing business with your organization for a long time.

- Keeping repeat customers saves your employer money by reducing the money spent on attracting new customers.

- Loyal clients often refer others to an organization's products and services, which creates opportunities to gain new customers.

Key Points

- Build better customer relationships by making good connections.

- Please get to know your customers and their needs and requirements.

- Think of customers as business partners with cooperative, mutually beneficial relationships.

- Communicate effectively to ensure good connections with customers.

Skill Practice

What did you notice?

What needed to be done correctly?

What could have been done?

Listening is Key

Course Description

Listening effectively to customers is decisive in successful customer service and retention. This online customer service training course aims to give customer service and call center representatives the basic skills they need to become good listeners. At the end of this training course, trainees will be able to understand the benefits of active listening to identify feelings, attitudes, and unspoken needs underlying customers' words, overcome listening obstacles, and use listening skills for outstanding customer care.

Why "The Power of Listening" Matters
- Listening is a natural human function and a skill that can be improved through training and practice.

- Research suggests people spend more time listening at work than other activities such as talking, reading, or writing.

- Listening allows customer service representatives to obtain essential customer information and identify their problems and complaints.

- Customer service representatives with good listening skills are likely to help their employers resolve conflicts and avoid legal trouble and costly lawsuits from angry, dissatisfied customers.

- Customer service representatives can learn about ways to improve their organization and its products through listening to feedback from customers.

Key Points

- Listening is an essential part of any job.

- With practice and determination, listening obstacles can be overcome, and you can become a more effective listener.

- Active listening requires the use of all senses.

- The more you listen, the better able you will be to meet and exceed customer expectations.

Skill Practice

What did you notice?

What needed to be done correctly?

What could have been done?

Soft Skills

Course Description

Telephone skills are among the most critical competencies customer service representatives need to be effective in their jobs and satisfy customers. The main objective of this online customer service training course is to cover the basic phone skills needed to be a successful customer service or call center representative. At the end of this course, trainees can answer the phone professionally and effectively, handle transfers and holds successfully, make the most of opportunities to call customers and take phone orders accurately and efficiently.

Why "Soft Skills" are important

- Most customer care representatives perform a significant portion of their work on the phone.

- How customer service representatives deal with customers on the phone—whether answering calls, making calls, handling phone orders, or using transfers and holds—often determines the success of customer interactions and customer satisfaction with your organization.

- Most customers judge the customer service representative in the first couple of seconds of the conversation, and the customer's opinion of the representative impacts their opinion of the employer.

- Excellent telephone skills can create an opportunity to alert customers to special offers, cross-sell, make add-on sales, save customers money, and enhance customer satisfaction.

- Customer service representatives who improve their phone skills become more efficient. The lengths of calls are shorter, customers are more satisfied, and representatives can provide service to a more significant number of clients.

Key Points

- How you answer the phone significantly impacts the success of customer calls.

- Use transfers and holds only as a last resort.

- Take advantage of opportunities to call customers to improve customer satisfaction and increase sales.

- Handle phone orders carefully—without charges, there is no business.

Skill Practice

What did you notice?

What needed to be done correctly?

What could have been done?

Earning and Keeping Your Clients' Trust

Course Description

To be successful and profitable, any business must keep satisfying its customers so that they keep coming back to do business. Loyal customers are the core of every business. This online customer loyalty and retention training course aims to help customer service representatives understand the importance of customer loyalty and discover ways to promote it. At the end of this course, trainees will be able to recognize the value of loyal customers, understand how to build and maintain loyalty, identify and meet customer expectations, and provide superior service that generates loyalty.

Why "Earning and Keeping Your Clients' Trust" is important

- Customers have more choices and are more demanding than ever. They can go to the competition if they don't get the kind of treatment they expect from one business.

- It can cost five times more to attract new customers than to keep current ones. Costs include advertising and promotion, sales representatives' time and training, opening new account records, and other administrative expenses.

- Some experts estimate that an organization can boost profits by 100 percent by retaining just 5 percent more customers.

- Loyal customers provide free advertising when they tell others about their positive experiences with the organization. These referrals can bring in new customers who have the potential to become loyal customers.

- Every contact with customers counts. One frustrating or unpleasant experience could be enough to turn a customer away from even the best product at the best price.

Key Points

- Without customers, we have no business.

- Customer loyalty is built on satisfaction.

- We rely on loyal customers to make our business successful.

- Every customer contact ensures satisfaction and builds customer loyalty.

Becoming a Better You

Course Description

With our customers, we would be in business and have jobs. That's why it is essential for every employee in every department of every workplace to develop a customer-oriented focus and always provide excellent service. This online customer service training course's main objective is to teach employees how to improve the service they provide to customers. By the time this course is over, employees should be able to recognize that we all have customers and share responsibility for customer satisfaction, understand what customers expect from them, handle customers' problems effectively, and help improve overall customer satisfaction.

Why "Becoming a Better You" is important
- Keeping repeat customers saves your employer money by reducing the amount spent on attracting new customers.

- Loyal clients often refer others to an organization's products and services, which creates opportunities to gain new customers.

- Dissatisfied customers tell as many as 20 other people about their experience. A strong customer focus at your workplace can minimize or prevent this problem.

- No matter the job, all employees have internal, external, or both customers.

Key Points

- All of us have customers—internal, external, or both.

- You play an essential role in ensuring customer satisfaction.

- When internal customers are satisfied, our organization runs at peak efficiency.

- When external customers are satisfied, they keep doing business with us.

- We all depend on satisfied customers for our continued success and prosperity.

Customer Service - How to Promote Among Staff Training

Course Description

To exist, every business needs customers. To thrive, companies need repeat and loyal customers. This means that all supervisors and employees must provide excellent customer care to external customers and the people within the organization who offer service. This online customer service training course aims to prepare supervisors to train and encourage their employees to provide all customers with the highest level of service. At the end of this training session, supervisors will be able to recognize that all employees have customers, understand what customers expect from their employees, create a customer-oriented focus in their department, and train employees to deal effectively with customers' problems and improve overall customer satisfaction.

Why "Customer Service - How to Promote Among Staff Training" Matters

- Studies repeatedly show that companies with high service quality garner a more significant market share and greater profits than those who fail to emphasize customer service.

- All employees have customers. Even if they don't work in customer service or deal directly with the company's customers, they have internal customers.

- Employees must also be able to resolve customers' problems successfully to exceed expectations. Customers appreciate a genuine effort to handle a situation, even when it can't be resolved satisfactorily. Solving an external customer's problem will usually increase loyalty to the organization. It is essential to solve customer issues to ensure they take their business elsewhere.

- It can cost up to five times more to attract new customers than to keep current ones. And competition for customers becomes stiffer every year in a challenging global market.

- Loyal customers help attract new customers. When they are happy doing business with an organization, they recommend its products and services to other people, which is free advertising.

- Satisfied customers are more likely to be loyal to the organization and less likely to complain or enter into disputes with the organization that could end up in court.

Attitudes for Service

The basis of a healthy customer service atmosphere is to give every customer an unparalleled experience, meet each customer's needs, and be a customer advocate.
Utilizing the tools given (helpfulness, genuine interest, and respect), escalating calls, and making customers comfortable knowing you will work to meet their needs.

Assess Customer
- Service Attitudes to set goals for improvement
- Incorporate the Four Drivers of Customer Service to build customer relationships.
- Apply Attitude Control Principles to manage their attitudes
- Use conversational language to keep the interaction low-pressure

Key Factors
- Attitude— Maintains a friendly, positive, and enthusiastic outlook.
- External Awareness— Sees things from multiple points of view. Keeps up to date with issues that affect responsibility.
- Customer Experience— Leverages positive experiences to create customer loyalty and long-term relationships.
- Stress Management— Differentiates between positive and negative stress. Maintains a balanced attitude.
- Interpersonal Skills— Displays a consistent ability to build solid relationships inside and outside the organization.

- Communication— Practices active listening supported with meaningful oral and written information.
- Influence— Consistently directs situations and inspires people for an all-win environment.
- Adaptability— Open-minded. Demonstrates flexibility when faced with changes at work.

Resolving Complaints

When clients complain, it will only be one of two reasons: emotional and rational. Resolving complaints requires dealing with both by clarifying complaints, lowering anxiety for both parties, using practical guidelines, and applying a process that deals with both emotional and rational factors to build even stronger customer relationships.

In this module, you will be able to explore the causes of complaints, identify ways to neutralize negative attitudes and follow a process that deals with complaints' emotional and rational elements. You will create approaches to maintaining a positive attitude, even when dealing with difficult people and issues. Protests don't have to be negative experiences all the time. You will work together to create win-win relationships with customers. You will examine the root causes of the complaints you receive and develop ways to reduce or eliminate them. Finally, you will discover that effectively resolving complaints is actually a way to reduce stress, build relationships, and improve customer loyalty and retention.

- Conflict Resolution— Bring people together who have been separated by their differences.
- Customer Experience— Leverages positive experiences to create customer loyalty and long-term relationships.
- Attitude— Maintains a friendly, positive, and enthusiastic outlook.
- Stress Management— Differentiates between positive and negative stress. Maintains a balanced attitude.

- Interpersonal Skills— Displays a consistent ability to build solid relationships inside and outside the organization.
- Communication— Practices active listening supported with meaningful oral and written information.

Objectives
- Deal with emotional and rational aspects of complaints
- Apply methods to reduce their stress when resolving complaints
- Implement a consistent process to resolve complaints
- Reduce the number and type of complaints received

Telephone Service

Today, more shopping is done online and over the telephone. Retail stores often have more phone calls than customers, so telephone service should be better than face-to-face service. When you receive a call, it is for a specific reason, and it is up to you to make sure before the customer hangs up the telephone you made a connection, engaged, and informed. There is an old saying: "You never get a second chance to make a first impression." When you answer the telephone, you only have seconds to make an impression on the customer. With that said, let us look at meaningful ways to enhance the telephone service experience.

Don't Miss The Chance to Impress
- Believe it or not, the person on the other end of the telephone can hear your smile, body language, and attitude. (Skill Practice)

- Positive energy is contagious! Those around you and individuals on the telephone can feed off your positive energy.

- Make sure you end your greeting with your name. This allows the customer to connect with you.

- Let the customer do most of the talking. When you respond, ensure it has relevant information and a warm and inviting tone.

Use Pleasantries
- This is the time to be professional and show your expertise (promotions, clearances, sales, new products, etc.).

- There is power in words! Ensure you are using Please, Thanks, Great, Perfect, super, Excellent, etc.

- The more times you can say YES, the more settled and unyielding the customer becomes.

Engagement Is Key

- Ask for the customer's name after offering information to the individual on the other end of the telephone. This builds relationships and respect.
- The call is personal once you and the customer address each other by name.
- The connection is strengthened.

Make Sure You Ask Open-ended Ended Questions

- Open-ended questions keep the customer from answering Yes or No. i.e., How may I help you? What styles are you looking for today?

- Open-ended questions keep the customer from having a guard up.

- Open-ended questions allow you to gather information and be professional.

- Opened questions keep you ahead of the customer

- Open-ended questions allow you to service the customer best.

Pay Close Attention to Interests

- When offering information (sales, promotion, clearances, new products), listen for signals of interest.

- Examples of signals of interest are: Really? Wow! I didn't know that., etc.

- Make sure to ask the customer questions to get a commitment, "How does that sound?" How does this sound compared to other offers you received? Etc.

Seal the Deal

- Ask the customer, "When are you planning to come in? Will we see you today? Etc

- Make sure to inform of the timeframe of promotions.

- Create urgency to take advantage.

- Give directions when asked.

- Inform the customer to ask for you when they arrive. This continues the relationship and engagement.

- Close with the customer's name as well as yours.

Skill Practice

What did you notice?

What needed to be done correctly?

What could have been done?

www.ingramcontent.com/pod-product-compliance
Lightning Source LLC
Chambersburg PA
CBHW050816160726
48004CB00002B/873